# GAME FACE

## GOALIE MASK COLORING BOOK

by Russell Field

ILLUSTRATED BY
Ross Garrison

SOMERVILLE HOUSE, USA
NEW YORK

Copyright © 1999 Somerville House Books Limited
and NHL Enterprises, L.P.

ISBN: 1-58184-035-7    A B C D E F G H I J

Printed in Canada

Writer: Russell Field
Illustrator: Ross Garrison
Designer: fiwired.com

Somerville House, USA is distributed by
Penguin Putnam Books for Young Readers,
345 Hudson Street, New York, N.Y. 10014

Published in Canada by Somerville House Publishing
a division of Somerville House Books Limited
3080 Yonge Street, Suite 5000
Toronto, ON
M4N 3N1

e-mail: sombooks@goodmedia.com
Web site: www.sombooks.com

Photographs
cover Al Bello/Allsport
page 1 Hockey Hall of Fame
page 2 left, Hockey Hall of Fame
page 2 right, Imperial Oil - Turkofsky, Hockey Hall of Fame
page 3 left, Imperial Oil - Turkofsky, Hockey Hall of Fame
page 3 right, Bruce Bennett Studios
page 4 upper, B. Bennett/Bruce Bennett Studios
page 4 lower, Harry Scull/Allsport
page 5 left, Hockey Hall of Fame
page 5 right, J. Leary/Bruce Bennett Studios
page 6 top row left to right, B. Winkler/Bruce Bennett Studios; J. Giamundo/Bruce Bennett Studios
page 6 bottom row left to right, W. Roberts/Bruce Bennett Studios; Stephen Dunn/Bruce Bennett Studios; Lisa Meyer/Bruce Bennett Studios
page 7 top row left to right, Paul Angers/Bruce Bennett Studios; J. Giamundo/Bruce Bennett Studios; B. Bennett/ Bruce Bennett Studios
page 7 2nd row left to right, J. Leary/Bruce Bennett Studios; W. Roberts/ Bruce Bennett Studios; J. Giamundo/Bruce Bennett Studios
page 7 bottom row left to right, Brian Winkler/ Bruce Bennett Studios; J. Leary/Bruce Bennett Studios; Jim McIsaac/Bruce Bennett Studios; Al Bello/Allsport
page 8 top row left to right, J. Giamundo/Bruce Bennett Studios; J. Giamundo/Bruce Bennett Studios; J. Giamundo/Bruce Bennett Studios; J. Giamundo/ Bruce Bennett Studios
page 8 2nd row left to right, J. McIsaac/Bruce Bennett Studios; J. McIsaac/Bruce Bennett Studios; Joe Patronite/Pinnacle '97; Brian Bahr/Allsport
page 8 bottom row left to right, M. Backner/ Bruce Bennett Studios; J. McIsaac/Bruce Bennett Studios; J. Giamundo/Bruce Bennett Studios; J. Leary/Bruce Bennett Studios

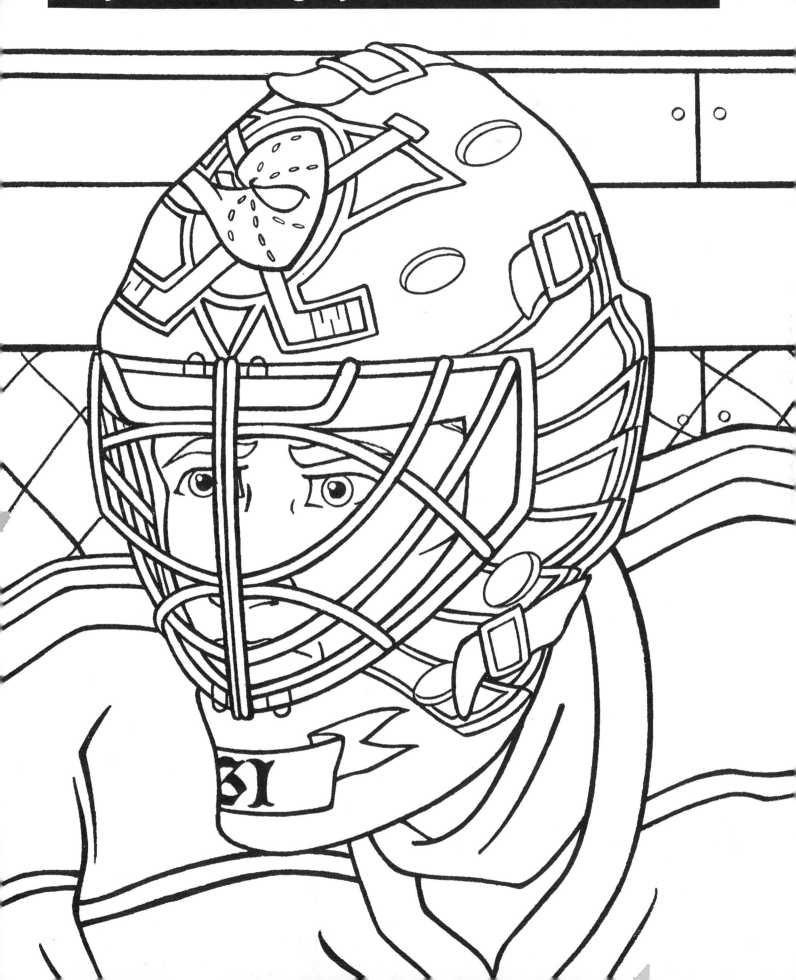

Byron Dafoe's Boston Bruins Mask

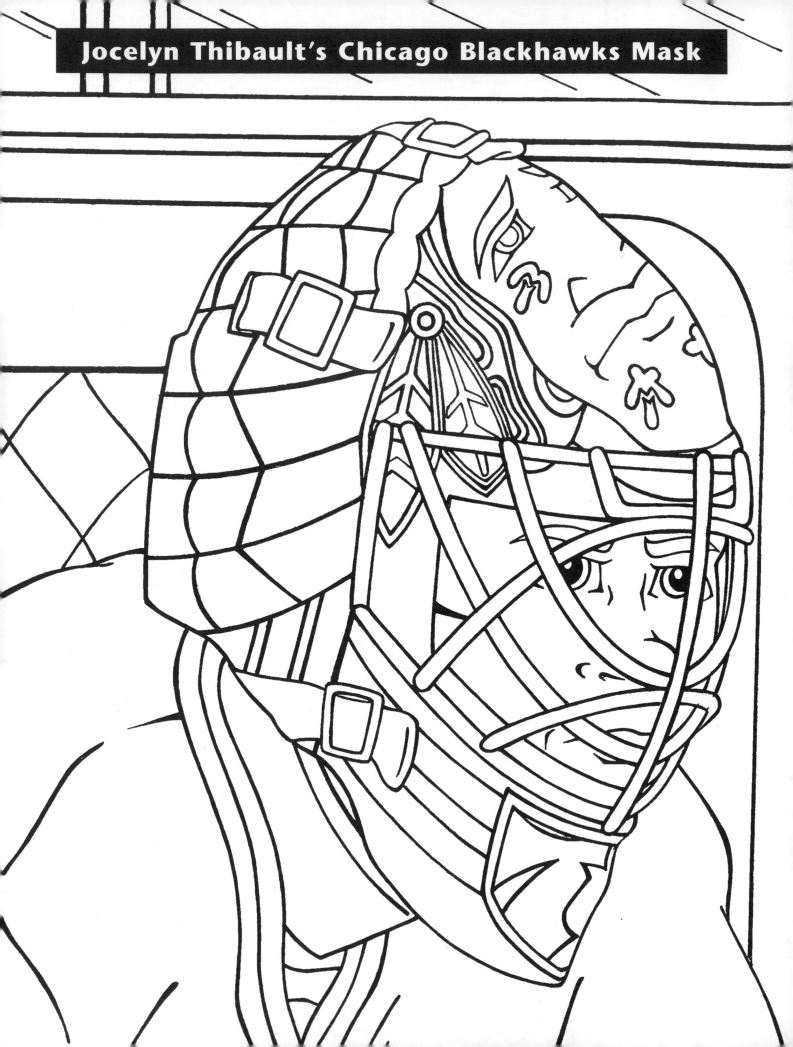

Roman Turek's Dallas Stars Mask

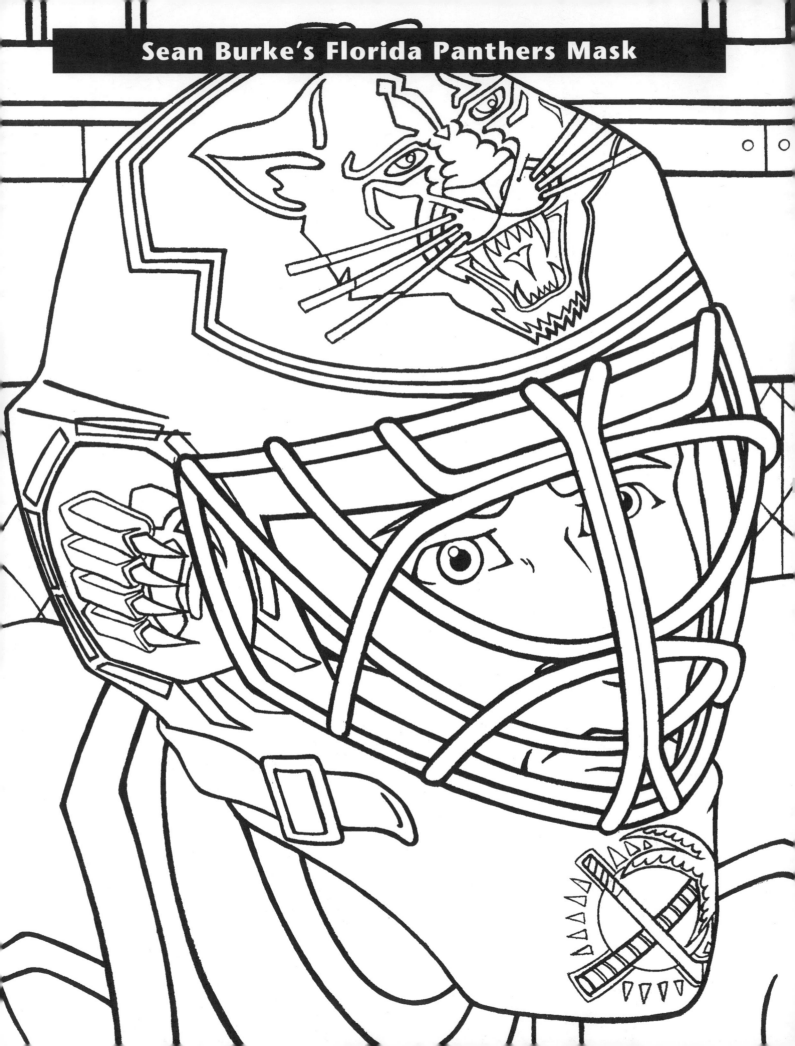

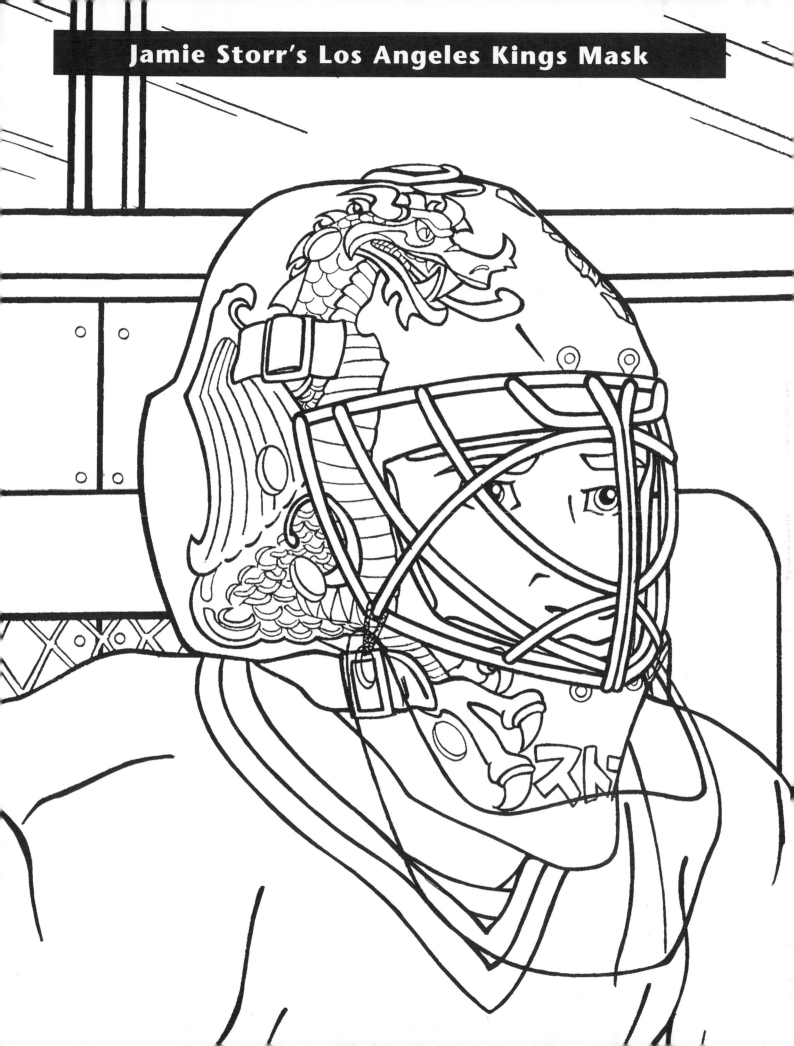

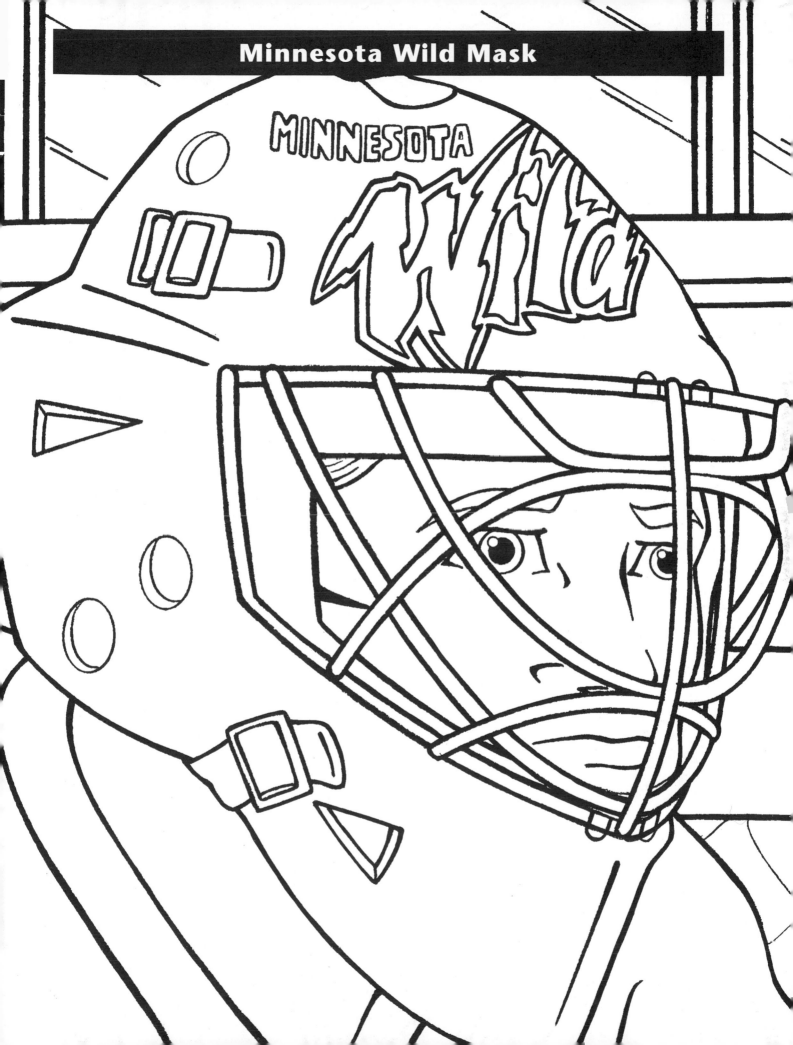

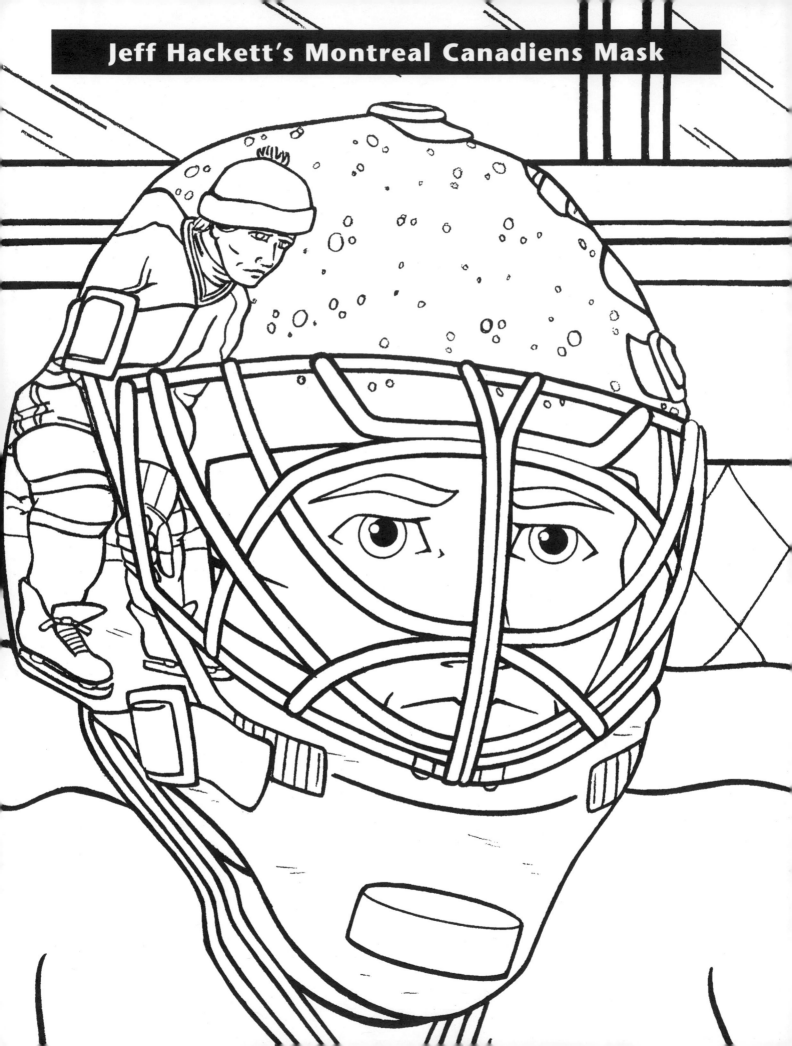

# GAME FACE

## GOALIE MASK COLORING BOOK

This book is all about goalie masks. Did you ever wonder why goalies wear a mask? There was a time when none of the goalies in the NHL wore a mask. That's right, *none of them!*

Now just imagine that you're an NHL goalie and Al MacInnis of the St. Louis Blues is in front of you. His slapshot is the hardest in the NHL. It flies through the air at more than 90 miles an hour. That's faster than your mom and dad drive the car!

If Al MacInnis takes a slapshot at you, you want to stop the puck so he doesn't score, but you also want to be protected. Like all NHL goalies, you would wear pads to protect your legs, a chest protector to cover your body, and gloves on your hands. Of course, you would also want something to protect your face. That's why the goalie mask was invented.

Turk Broda
without a mask

## Where Did the Mask Come From?

The first goalie to wear a mask was a man named Clint Benedict, who played for a team called the Montreal Maroons. In a game in the late 1920s, a shot hit Benedict in the face and broke his nose.

Back in those days, teams only carried one goalie, and since it takes a while for a broken nose to heal, Benedict had to find a way to protect his sore nose during the Maroons' next game. So, he had a leather-and-wire mask made. The mask looked really scary, but Benedict had trouble seeing out of it, so he never wore it again.

## The Original "Jake the Snake"

It was over 30 years before another goalie wore a mask. That goalie's name was Jacques Plante. Plante's nickname was "Jake the Snake" and he was the star goalie for the Montreal Canadiens. Plante was always getting hit in the face with the puck, so he designed a mask made out of a very hard material called fiberglass. The mask was shaped like his face, with holes cut out for his eyes and nose.

The original mask worn by Jacques Plante

Clint Benedict's first mask

## Masks, Masks, Masks

Plante's coach didn't want him to wear the mask. No other goalie in the NHL wore one, so the coach didn't see why Plante should. On November 1, 1959, the Canadiens played the New York Rangers and a shot hit Plante in the face, cutting him.

The game was stopped and Plante refused to play again unless he was allowed to wear his mask. His coach had no choice and said okay. Plante went on to win the game so the coach allowed him to keep wearing the mask.

Over the years, there have been many different kinds of masks. Jacques Plante wore at least seven different masks in his career. All Plantes masks were made of fiberglass and molded to cover his entire face.

Unfortunately, fiberglass masks weren't perfect. They pressed right up against a goalie's face. So, if the goalie got hit in the face with the puck, he didn't get cut — but the shot still really hurt.

Grant Fuhr

Jacques Plante

# A New Breed of Mask

To solve the problems with fiberglass masks, a new, less painful, kind of mask was invented. It is called the "cage" and it looked just like a player's helmet except that it had a wire cage over the front of it. This new design made it easier for the goalie to see, and if a shot hit him in the mask, it wouldn't hurt as much.

One of the best goalies in the NHL is Dominik Hasek of the Buffalo Sabres. He is one of the few goalies in the NHL who still wears a cage. Other goalies in the NHL don't like the cage because they say it moves around too much and they like the fit of the fiberglass mask better.

To combine the best of both, a combination mask, or hybrid, was invented. The hybrid has a wire cage in front of the goalie's eyes but uses fiberglass to fit the mask tightly around the goalie's head. There is also a lot of padding in the mask to help protect the goalie's face.

Dominik Hasek's "cage"

Mark Fitzpatrick wears a "hybrid" mask.

# Shoot to Win!

To qualify for the NHL® Open Net Sweepstakes, complete the reverse of this entry form and mail it to the address below, and you could be chosen as a lucky winner!

Mail all completed entry forms to:
Penguin Putnam Books for Young Readers
NHL® Open Net Sweepstakes
345 Hudson Street, New York, NY 10014

NHL

®

**The Prizes**

The Grand Prize Winner receives air travel (coach) for him/herself and a parent or guardian, hotel accommodations in Toronto, Canada for 2 nights (based on double occupancy) and tickets to the 2000 NHL® Award Ceremony. In addition, the winner will have his/her photo taken with an NHL star, tour the arena, and other VIP treatment. Grand prize includes $350 (U.S.) stipend for meals, taxis and incidentals on the trip. (No other expenses are included. Winner and companion are responsible for transportation to and from the airport. Reservations once made may not be changed. Approximate retail value of grand prize ($2,255 U.S.) varies depending on point of departure in the United States.) Fifty Runners Up will receive a genuine NHL autographed hockey stick. (Approximate retail value is $75 U.S. per stick.)

**How to Enter and Eligibility**

NO PURCHASE NECESSARY. Enter by completing the official entry form (or by printing your name, address, age and phone number on a 3x5 card) and sending it in a business sized envelope to NHL® Open Net Sweepstakes, Penguin Putnam Inc., 345 Hudson Street, New York, NY 10014. No faxed entries will be accepted. Only one entry per envelope is permitted. Contest begins September 13, 1999. Entries must be received by January 1, 2000.

All contestants must be legal U.S. residents between the ages of 5 and 14 on January 1, 2000. Employees (and their families) of NHL Enterprises, L.P., NHL Enterprises, Canada, L.P., NHL Enterprises, B.V., the member clubs of the NHL (collectively the "NHL Entities"), Somerville House, USA and their respective affiliates, agencies, retailers, distributors, and advertising agencies, are not eligible to enter.

**Official Rules**

Winners will be selected the week of February 1, 2000 by a random drawing from all complete entries. Winners will be notified by mail on or around March 1, 2000. Odds of winning depend on number of entries received. Neither the NHL Entities nor Somerville House, USA is responsible for illegible entries or lost or misdirected mail. All entries become the property of Somerville House, USA and will not be returned. In the event there is an insufficient number of entries, Somerville House, USA reserves the right not to award all prizes. Judges decisions are final. Winners and their parents/legal guardians will be required to execute an affidavit of eligibility, a liability release, a publicity release and any other documentation that Somerville House, USA or NHL Entities require which must be returned within 14 days of notification or an alternative winner will be selected. Winners consent to the use of their name and/or photos or likeness for advertising and promotional purposes without additional compensation (except where prohibited). Taxes and fees are the sole responsibility of winners. Prizes cannot be transferred, redeemed for cash, or exchanged. Void where prohibited by law. All entrants are subject to, agree to comply with, and be bound by these rules. The NHL Entities, Somerville House, USA and their affiliates, officers, directors, employees, and agents shall not be liable for any claims related to this contest or any prize awarded. For the names of the winners, send a self-addressed stamped envelope to : NHL® Open Net Sweepstakes Winners, c/o Penguin Putnam Inc., 345 Hudson Street, New York, NY 10014.

Name _____

Age _____ phone # (optional) _____

Address _____

City _____

State _____ Zip Code _____

Entries must be received by January 1, 2000. Winners will be notified by mail on or about March 1, 2000

Mail all completed entry forms to:
Penguin Putnam Books for Young Readers
NHL® Open Net Sweepstakes
345 Hudson Street, New York, NY 10014

**1**
Grand
Prize Winner
will receive:
**a trip for 2
to the
2000 NHL®
Award Ceremony**

**50**
Runners-Up
will receive:
**a genuine
NHL®
autographed
hockey stick**

# It's Like a Piece of Art on Your Face

Whichever type of mask a goalie wears, it has to do three things. First, it has to protect his face. Second, it has to be comfortable. (That's why the cage mask was invented.) And, third, a mask must allow the goalie to see, otherwise he won't be able to stop the puck!

It's important that masks do all these things, but it's okay for masks to look cool, too! That's why some goalies have their masks painted.

The first goalie to paint his mask was Gerry Cheevers of the Boston Bruins. He painted stitches on his mask each time a puck hit him in the face. That way, he could show exactly where his mask had saved him from having to get stitches in his face.

Goalies paint all sorts of things on their masks. Many goalies have their team's logo and colors painted on their mask to show people that they really want to be part of their team.

Gerry Cheevers

Martin Brodeur

Some goalies, like Mike Richter have famous places painted on their mask to remind people where they play. Other goalies want really fierce animals painted on their masks to scare away other players. You wouldn't want to go near Godzilla, which is why Olaf Kolzig chose to paint Godzilla on his mask. Curtis Joseph of the Toronto Maple Leafs is nicknamed Cujo, which is the name of a scary dog in a Stephen King book! Cujo has a dog painted on his mask.

Using the photogaphs of all these cool masks, color in the drawings found in this book — either exactly like the real goalies, or in any wild colors you like!

**Guy Hebert**
Anaheim Mighty Ducks

Atlanta Thrashers

**Byron Dafoe**
Boston Bruins

**Ken Wregget**
Calgary Flames

**Trevor Kidd**
Carolina Hurricanes

**Jocelyn Thibault**
Chicago Blackhawks

**Patrick Roy**
Colorado Avalanche

Columbus Blue Jackets

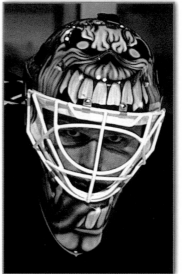

**Roman Turek**
Dallas Stars

**Sean Burke**
Florida Panthers

**Jamie Storr**
Los Angeles Kings

**Kelly Hrudey** (retired)
Los Angeles Kings

Minnesota Wild

**Jeff Hackett**
Montreal Canadiens

**Mike Dunham**
Nashville Predators

**Martin Brodeur**
New Jersey Devils

**Tommy Salo**
New York Islanders
(now with Edmonton Oilers)

**Mike Richter**
New York Rangers

**Damian Rhodes**
Ottawa Senators

**Ron Tugnutt**
Ottawa Senators

**John Vanbiesbrouck**
Philadelphia Flyers

**Nikolai Khabibulin**
Phoenix Coyotes

**Tom Barrasso**
Pittsburgh Penguins

**Peter Skudra**
Pittsburgh Penguins

**Kelly Hrudey** (retired)
San Jose Sharks (allstar)

**Mike Vernon**
San Jose Sharks

**Grant Fuhr**
St. Louis Blues

**Curtis Joseph**
Toronto Maple Leafs

**Garth Snow**
Vancouver Canucks

**Olaf Kolzig**
Washington Capitals

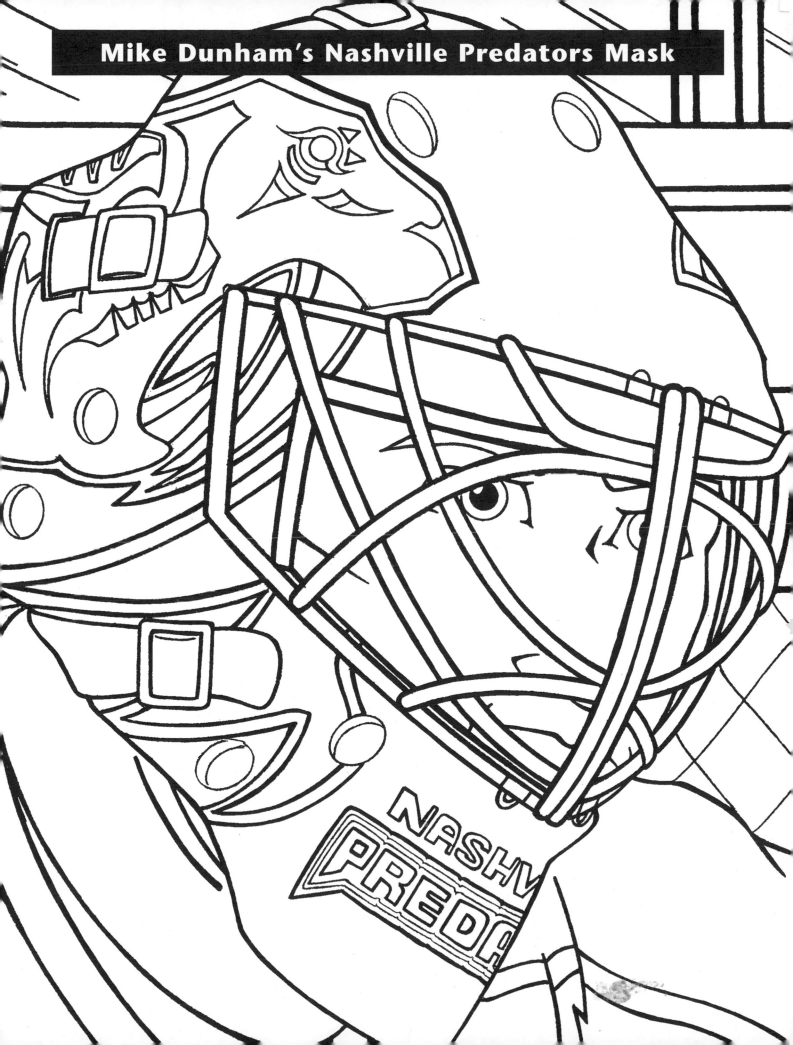

Martin Brodeur's New Jersey Devils Mask

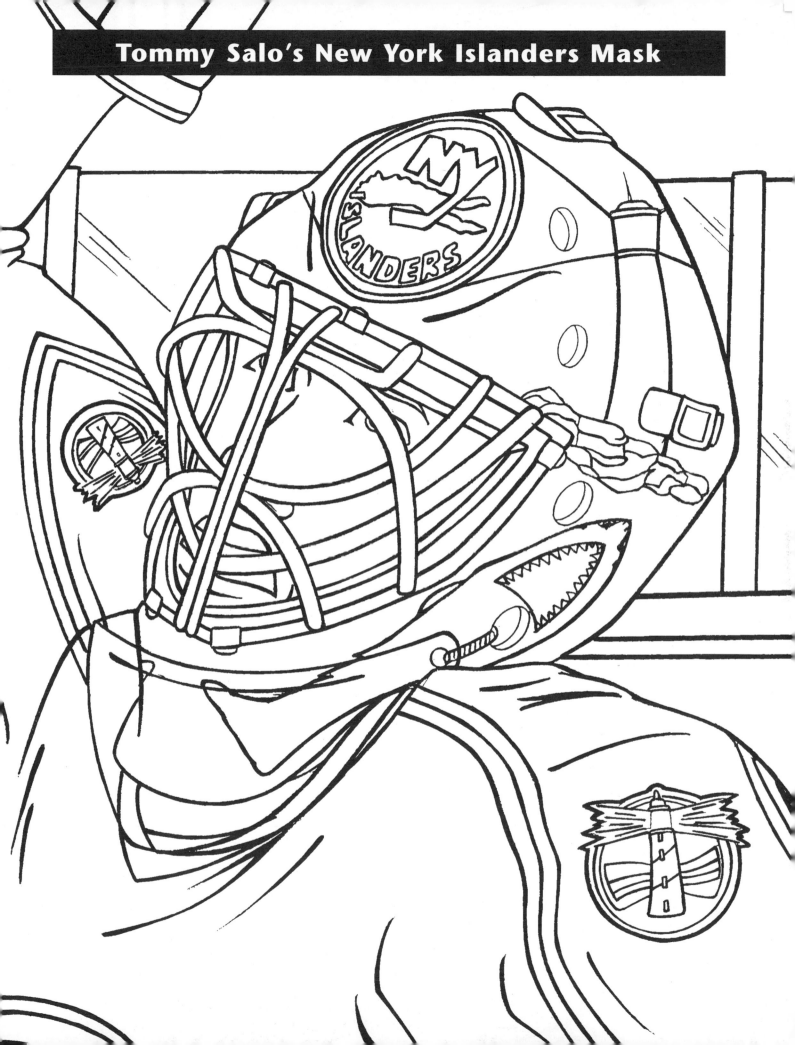

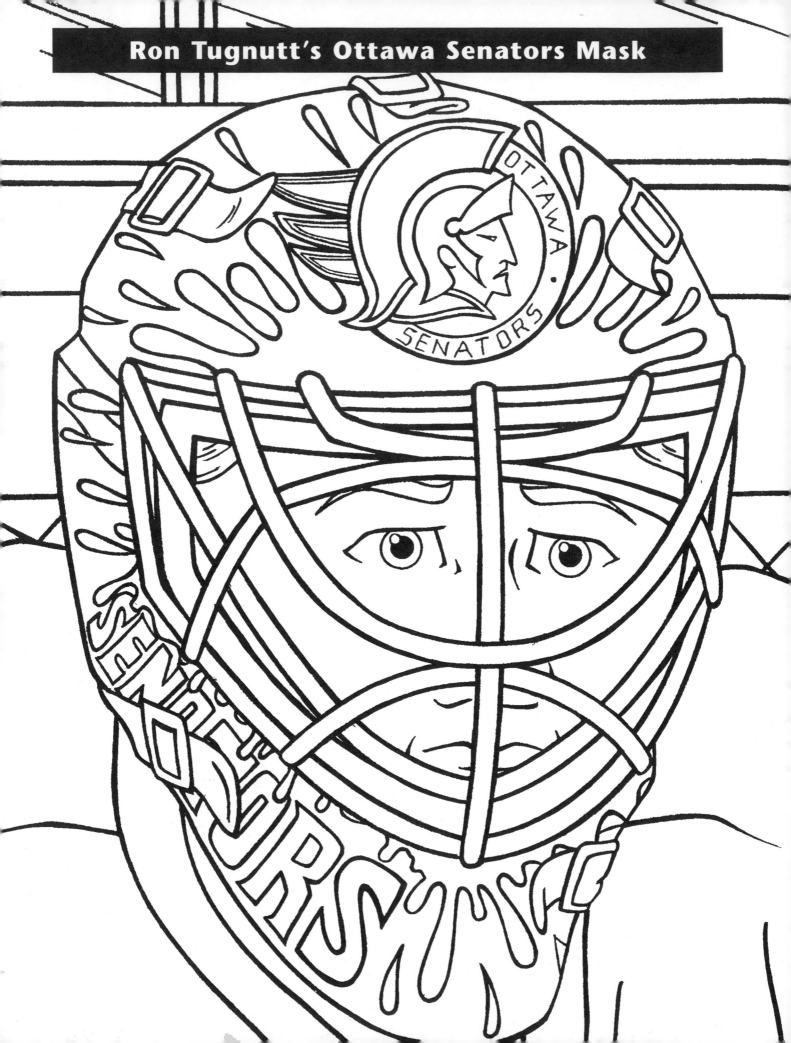

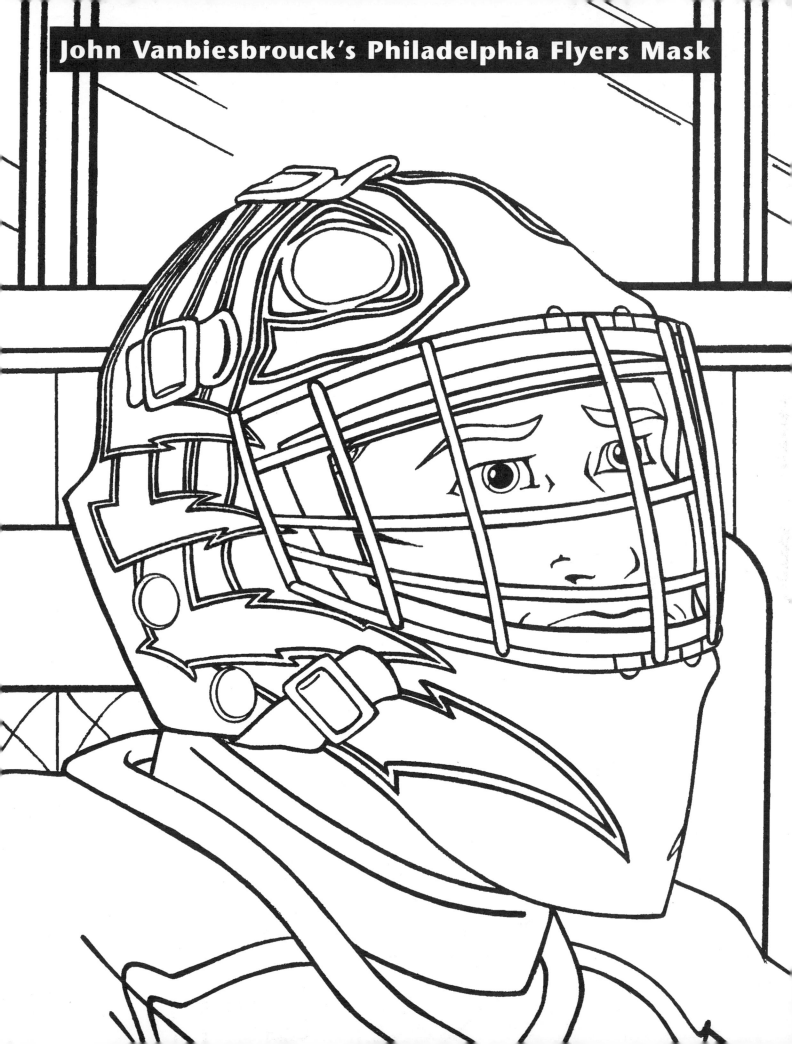

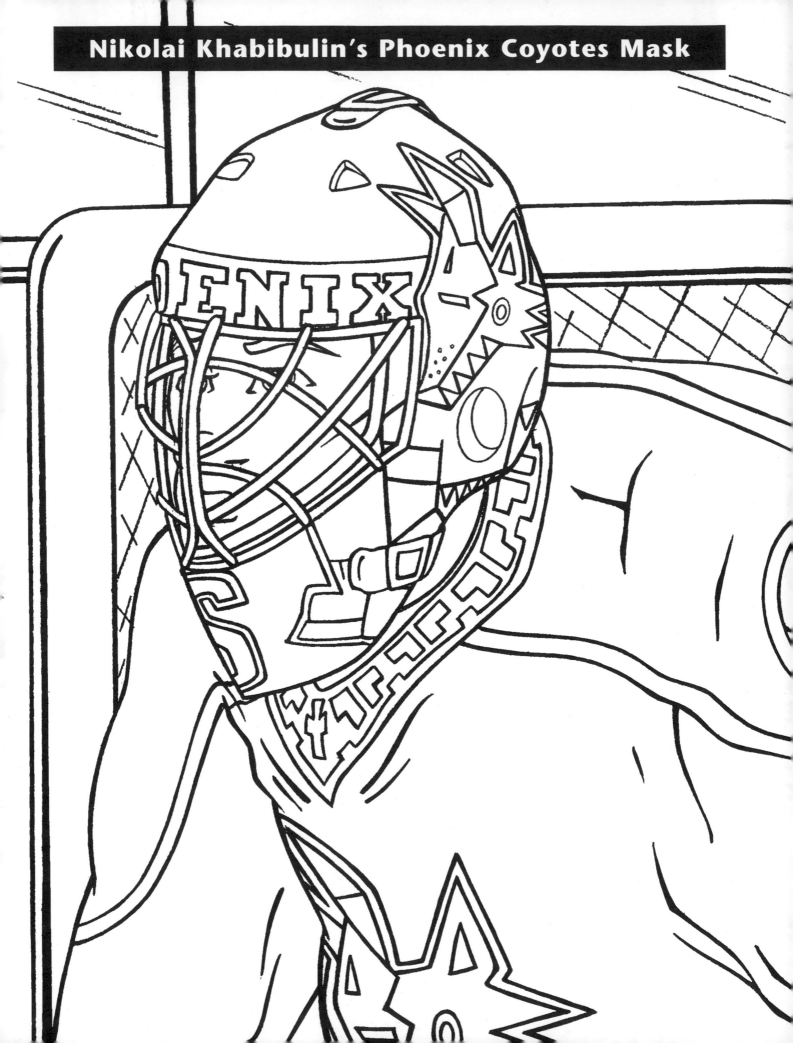

Nikolai Khabibulin's Phoenix Coyotes Mask

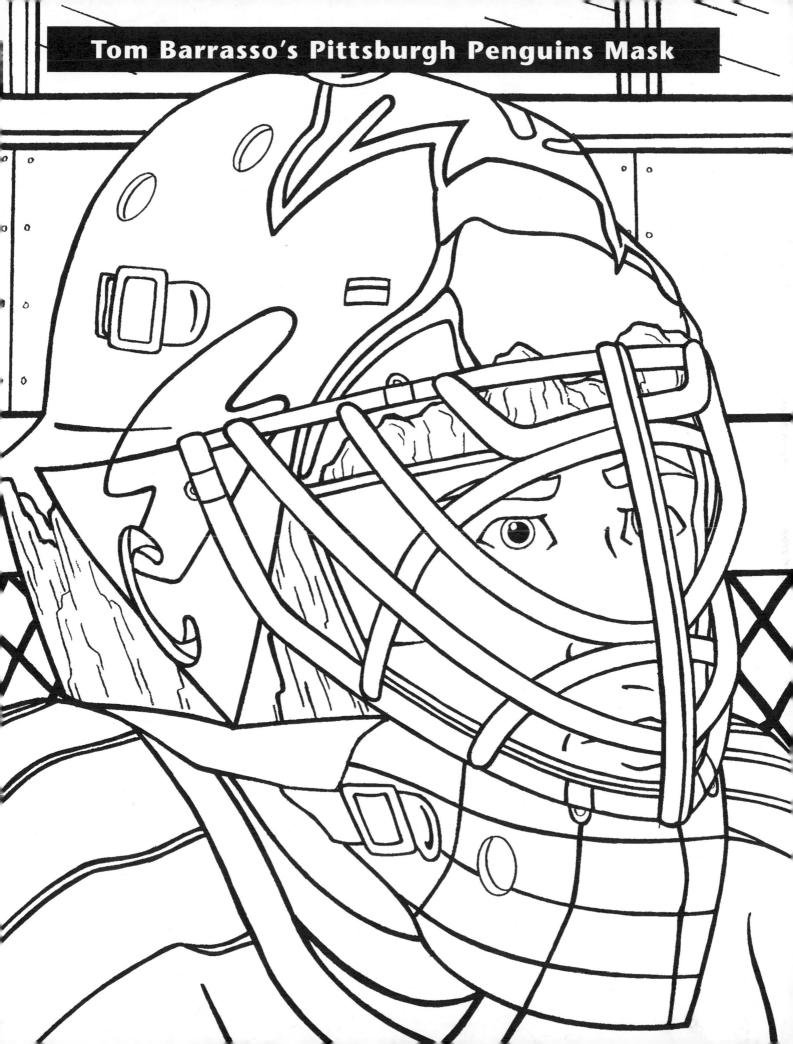

Tom Barrasso's Pittsburgh Penguins Mask

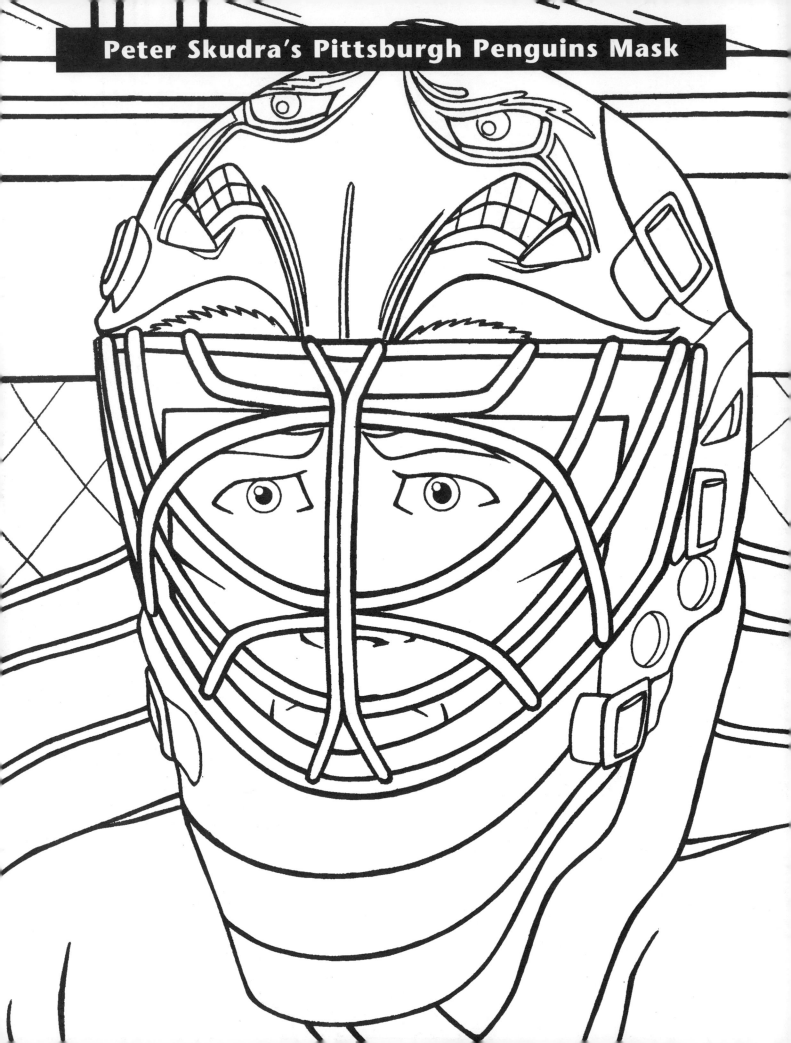

Peter Skudra's Pittsburgh Penguins Mask

Kelly Hrudey's 1997 All-Star Game Mask

Mike Vernon's San Jose Sharks Mask

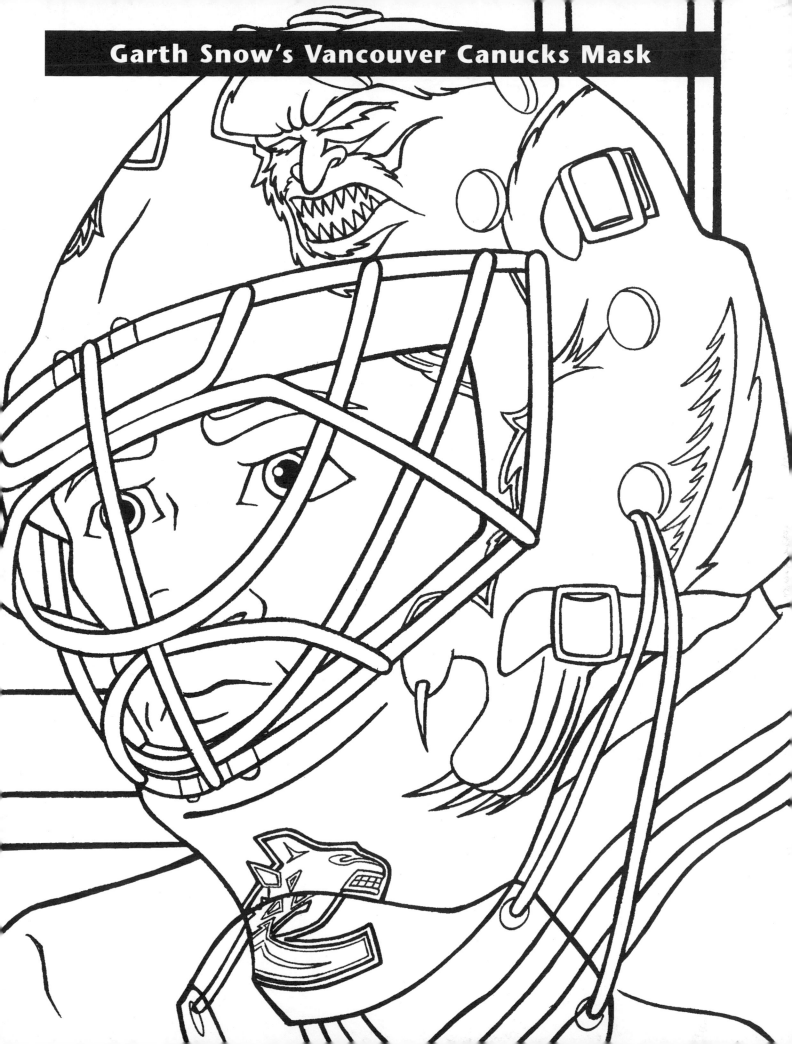

Olaf Kolzig's Washington Capitals Mask